THE WORLD IS
STILL LEARNING

THE WORLD IS STILL LEARNING

Lauren Mackenzie

To order additional copies of this book, contact:
Xlibris
1-888-795-4274
www.Xlibris.com
Orders@Xlibris.com
787516

CONTENTS

FOREWORD

In May of 2018, I saw Lauren walk across the stage to accept from me her Girl Scout Gold Award, the highest honor a Girl Scout can receive. Immediately I was struck by her poise and apparent self-confidence. Moreover, Lauren had completed her Award project as a high school sophomore, two years earlier than most young women. I sought out Lauren and her parents following the ceremony to say a personal congratulations and share my thoughts. It was only then that I learned that Lauren was someone special —less assured, but much deeper and more insightful than I had perceived. We undertook a friendship and mentoring relationship in which I knew I could help her with connections for potential summer jobs and college recommendations. However, I learned that she was a true poet and my time with Lauren blossomed into something much more.

Lauren's poetry in her book, The World Is Still Learning, is a window into pain, truth and hope that she has felt personally as well as what she has experienced through her empathetic journey of reading about others, friends and family. She has bravely taken on topics that distress young adults, teenagers, and so many others, including social injustice, abusive relationships, race relations, self-doubt, and mental health. Lauren's mother asked me, after I read an earlier manuscript, if the work was too raw and if Lauren should consider any changes. I told her what I am telling you now: in today's world, we need more real, more raw, more truth and more openness.

This book encompasses the reality of life through many thoughtful poems. Lauren's poetry connects with the reader by its authenticity and sharing experiences while whispering throughout its message that no one is alone. I commend to you this treasure of Lauren's passionate and poignant work. I hope it touches you as it did me.

Kit Addleman, JD
Board Chairwoman, Girl Scouts of Northeast Texas
Partner and Chair of the SEC Defense Practice, Haynes and
Boone, LLP

"The pain of youth, laid bare, and a new poetic voice for resilience and love of self and others. Lauren Mackenzie's poems offer an elegant meditation on the brutalities that Americans foist on each other and the interior struggles many live with. And yet her own victory over despair, evident in this book, offers hope that individuals and a country can rise above loathing, and choose love."

--Sheryll Cashin Author of Loving: Interracial Intimacy and the Threat to White Supremacy (Beacon, 2017)
Carmack Waterhouse Professor of Law, Civil Rights and Social Justice
Georgetown University Law Center
Vanderbilt '84 Oxford '86 Harvard Law School '89

"A well written set of poetry by a youth wise beyond her years, expressing both pain and hope wrapped in resilience and foresight that few more mature in age possess. Grounded in her faith, Lauren Mackenzie has reached into the depths of her young soul to expose the rough emotions and triumphs of life that offer hope to us all."

--Congresswoman Terri A. Sewell, U.S. Representative of Alabama's 7th Congressional District
Princeton '86 Oxford '88 Harvard Law School '92

"Lauren Mackenzie has produced an important work. Her poems are an honest portrait of what pain and hope looks and feels like to her generation. We are blessed that she had the courage to give voice to these moments. Thank you, Lauren. We are better because of this book of poems."

--Dr. Michael J. Sorrell
President of Paul Quinn College
Fortune Magazine: The World's 50 Greatest Leaders (2018)
Time Magazine: 31 People Changing the South (2018)
Duke Law School and University of Pennsylvania Ed.D

I hope the words in this book bring healing to your heart and peace to your soul. May your walk be confident, with power underneath your feet, knowing that your victory is attainable. As you begin your journey to self-acceptance and freedom know that we all are still learning that freedom is attainable. May the following pages, which represent the lives, of many young men and women, stir your heart and encourage you to free your mind. I hope the words I have written positively impact you and that the pages come alive opening your eyes to the pathway of the different lives we lead and separate from what we perceive our lives to be. I hope my words bring you a sense of stability and a sense of hope, knowing you are not alone.

With love,
Lauren Mackenzie

VOLUME 1

THE BEGINNING

Viridity
escapes the lips.

Binding, independent thought,
forcing silence to the lips.

Wickedness is taught,
not instilled in the mind.
Hands of innocence
still reach for stars in the sky.

Viridity escapes the lips.

Once a child's heart,
now tightened by a fiery grip.
Such soft beginnings,
touch yet unproclaimed.
Put on your dress-up; let's play a game.

Viridity escapes the lips.

Doll-sewed smiles,
clenched teeth,
pink lips,

People with secrets.
People with tricks.
Masqueraded appearances
can often hide the confidence that has been stripped.

Viridity escapes the lips.

City sounds blare.

Gun sounds drip.
Caved-in minds,
treading lies,
grow up quick so you can survive.

Viridity escapes the lips.

They watched as the surface traced a line of pits.
Sharp points overpower,
Addict by the hour.
The mind washes away the pain it encounters.

Viridity escapes the lips.

Pathways unknown,
lives left unfixed,

but innocence has not been expended.
It lives within the torn pages of our lives,
even when the mind tries to weaken us at the most defaced times.
But without adversity, how would we beget capacity?
Without awareness, develop change?

In the midst of a disfigured world, we have the power to bring unity.

We are the children.
Yes we are smitten,
only because our emergence precipitates discrimination.

We are the children.
Do black hoods make us villains?
Does skin influence society's events of misconstruance?

We are the children.
Shot down for no reason
because of the voices that denounce our hopes as unfathomable of reaching.

We are the children.
Lying in coffins of indictment
and prejudiced views.
Living the sacrifice of unchanged history,
sometimes paying the price in coffins underground too.

We are the children.
Chains of baggage
ingrained in our frame.
So how are we to propel
when blood ties our hands to the destiny of being enslaved?

Yet,
we are still the children.
Subsisting of high expectations,
a generation of new steps and new formation.

We are the children.
The children you will see,
because society will not hinder us from being completely free.
We are the generation of youth, a generation armed in power.

Viridity does not stay.
Birth does not taint.
It is what we are born into that ruins our clean slate.

Innocent lives,
with innocent minds,
uncountable stars danced by in the sky.

The oceans below,
They trembled and roared,
Holding our drowning souls that were yearning for more.

But we will survive.
Even when life often drowns us as we search for the other side.

But we must keep swimming,
even when the waves try to hold us down.

We must keep swimming
even when hope is neither lost or found.

We must keep swimming
because soon we will find
our dreams becoming reality right before our eyes.

They were just on the other side of the ocean.

Tell me, *dear society*,
is today a truth or a lie?
Should we continue to create a world
that tells others to cover up the wounds they hold inside?

If we begin to condone a movement of vulnerability,
breaking down the walls of judgment and insensitivity,
we then can begin to create a society of support that makes
others feel apart instead of alone.

I walk these halls.
Seas of people
who don't know me at all.

Patched smiles upon the face.
Hiding pain,
hiding hate,

hide the fear of being pushed away.

Have you looked for the girl?
Eyes filled with strife.

Have you looked past the boy?
Broken seams, solemn eyes.

It's a shame we're inept to characterize past the surface of the
skin,
because if we could, maybe we'd realize that everyone is hurting
within.

Gun sounds dripped.
Walls caved in.

Pull the alarm.

Rain pours down hard.

Chaotic running.

Trigger keeps clicking.

Bang, bang, bang.

Bullets wrapped in hate.
Bullets wrapped in pain,
but cold eyes can't mask his face of pain.

Seventeen shots.

Bang, bang, bang.

Blood fills the room.
Sirens ring.

Fear fills the air.
Footsteps approach.
Hiding bodies, he thinks.
It's time to play hide and seek.

Loneliness envelops him.
Violence destroys him.
Animosity filled him.
Now he wants corruption.

Gushing tears,
muffled cries,
short texts of futile good-byes.
Who are we to blame?
Society, I would say?
If we loved and did not hate,
would he pull the trigger?

Happy eyes.
Floating on lies.
Carnival lights reflect in my eyes.
Cotton candy pink.
No fear,
no weep,
but quickly many realize children are mean.

Wails of pain.
Laughter brings shame.
Rocks hit knees.
Fists bring spleens.
Tumbling down steps.
Wounds infected and unkept.

Loneliness can often feel like the only option left.

Sitting still
on the merry-go-round.

Tears drowning out the bitter sounds.

Playground tales.

For many, not the happiest of stories.

But children reflect what they see, meaning if the world reflected kindness,
would our community of youth's reactions often be less mean?

Bodies engulfed in shades of blue.
Torn, beaten, killed, and bruised,
black innocent souls,
bullets pierced through their bones.
Can we hide the perception that depreciates our souls?

We must disregard outer perception and deprogram our eyes
to no longer see a color. Whether black or blue, we must come
together.

Many want love.
Many want acceptance
because the world gives us a disfigured impression.

Humankind constructs
what is not the norm,
leaving those who are different feeling abandoned and scorned.

People change,
to simply be accepted.
Eating lies,
persisting correction.

We all have a vision of what we believe would make us utter
perfection.
Insecurities are embedded in all of us.
Many you would never, ever think of.

Shattered mirrors.
Shattered fears.
Shattered shapes
and blistering tears.

Distorted eyes.
See boundless lies.
Am I enough?
Never,
the voice replies.

Sickly obsessions,
gnawing perceptions,
skipping meals
because scales do degrade.

Angry fist shatter
the numerous mirrors that cause pain.

Fingers down throat.
Streams of release.
Am I enough?
Reflections ask again in defeat.

We are enough, so we must look in the mirrors that broke us and tell them
that's enough.
Each face, each soul and body, is a work of art.
So why do we listen to the standards of an unjust society?
We were not made for perfection.
We were made to be human.
Know you are beautiful, and never forget.

Perception overrides realism,
harming the realist eye.
Solicitude is felt
for the ones with unveiled, yet cloaked eyes.

Tenderly protected by ignorant perspective,
throttling the brain,
formulating misconception.

Societal standards
on human acceptance.
The world gives us a twisted reflection.

Ideal beauty is unreal in itself.
Media's perception
softly guides the soul to hell.

The mouth is force fed
both cheesy truths and appealing lies.
Tell us, society,
how are we to love ourselves when at the same time,
you encourage us to hunger to live up to your distorted lies?

Civilizations categorize
grouping people in stereotypes of lies.

Humanity is hurting,
losing empathy,
one step at a time.

People recite rhymes,
tell others to handle what's inside.
Then they wonder why people want to fly high above the sky.
We wonder why drugs replace utter demise.
We wonder why death is a result for peace
because society makes peace unachievable to the broken, it
seems.

I am sorry to the people who feel like death is a game,
constantly juggling with life like a card game.

People that lost their lives
because of the torment inside their minds.

Because of the words that pushed them to the edge.
Because of the way society continues to put these topics up on
the ledge.

Society has brought this down upon innocent lives.
I am sorry that the system of life isn't always right.

Like many, I believe we all have a dream.
A dream that peace would multiply, like an incessant sea.
A dream that as people, we all would be free.
But what is freedom if the declaration already says we are indeed?

Like MLK,
I have a dream,
a dream that defines what it is to be free.
A vision that as people we would unveil our eyes and see.
That humanity is diminishing and society is still not free.

Pompous stares and embellowing perceptions.
Ridiculous standards that cause unacceptance.

Kindness should be uplifted,
hearts unseeded of narrowed views.
As people we should conceptualize that we have no room for biased views.

When people are in need,
cruelty churns like a sea.
Numerous people caught in the vicious cycle of wealth and greed.

Human hearts in need of liberation
instead of sick-minded views,
we need empathy to replace condemnation.

I have a dream
that forgiveness would flood,
that people would not have to fear people anymore.

Free from the mind-set that keeps us wrapped and in need.
Free from the feeling that drugs will make you free.

I have a dream that color would not be attached to beauty.
Differences not to imbalance.
Stereotypes unattached to the being of someone's soul.

Beliefs that keep us separated.
Religions and cultures divided.
Narrowed ways of the world that keep people in fear to be who they are.

I have a dream
that we will join hands together,
knowing that change starts with us coming together.
That people won't look at others pain and judge but instead know they are
hurting and help them overcome.

Though there is so much in the world that needs to be changed,
I will start with this dream,
this dream of change.

So like Martin Luther King, I have a dream,
a dream that we all would truly step in the belief that everyone deserves to be
completely free.

VOLUME 2
THE LEARNING

I draw air through my lungs.
Sun caresses my skin.
Warmth tingles down my spine.
Butterflied hearts and gentle wind,
freeing my mind.
Can I finally trust this time?

Though my heart wants,
my soul shrieks at the thought.
The translucent glass shatters.
Flooding thoughts do not stop.
Memories push through my mind.
I instantaneously speed back into time.

Haunting shadows.
Silent screams.
One touch.
I cannot breathe.

Choking on words,
my limbs tremble in fear.
I wake up to realize, I escaped into my own nightmares.

Concerned eyes.
What just happened in the mind?
Will I have to explain each and every time?

When we realize we have the strength to not allow our past to hold us down,
we will take one step toward the journey of freedom.

Music blasting.
Teeth chattering.
Smells of apprehension
ascend.

Swigs of liquid.
Laughter echoes.
Fire fills the lungs within.

Heat rises.
Eyes deaden.
Down a cherry coke,
when the rush kicks in.

Factitious freedom and contrived glee.
Dizzy bodies and deceiving eyes besiege me.

Escape.

Escape.

Escape.

Is everyone doing this because of self-hate?

This does not help the pain.

I loved.
I loved too hard.
I fell in love with the cherry-blossom trees,
the way their branches swayed in the breeze.
I fell in love with starry skies, teething smiles, and painful eyes.
I fell in love with empty pages,
smearing my heart
across the pages.
I fell in love with an appealing mask,
hiding my destroyed face of wrath.
I fell in love with broken souls, broken beings, and broken
shores.

As I desperately dug my hands in the sand,
holding on, hoping it was not too late for me to take flight and
then land,
stars fell at my feet.
The oceans roared in the wind.
And in this moment, I realized I had fallen in love
with everything, but myself.

Cliff ahead.
I walk towards the edge.

At the top of the sea,
the stars envelop me.

As I lie placid,
looking at *violescent* skies,
I know I must keep going in life.

I must get to the other side.

violescence.
The mixed emotions of tranquility and turmoil.

Night poured into my eyes.
Whistles and chatter, I climb to the top of the ladder,
skies painted velvet blue.
Deep lavender winds stir and brew.
I was an angel, one with city buildings and glistening lights,
looking down below watching bustling cars zip by.
Fingertips outstretched,
hand touched mine.
"Jump," you said.
"You'll feel alive."
My feet took flight.
I swear I flew in the midst of the night,
lifted or maybe unknowingly falling down.
My feet hit cement, suddenly touching the ground.
I looked to see you smile.
You beckoned for us to jump again.
But these were the moments before you lost your soul within.

The moments before everything bad began.

Ocean waters float calmly in my mind.
One wave crashes as the other subsides.
I believed in the stars.
The stars in my mind,
the ones that kept me afloat and drowned the sorrows inside.
Life will be a process of falling in deep waters. If it takes
drowning numerous times keep swimming till you are able to
see the other side. Be patient, for one day you will be able to run
on waters while everyone else is walking on land.

Transparent skies,
treading water,
bare feet,
waters rise high,
swallow many in defeat.

You can die or drown.
Swim or sail.
It's the mind's
process of thinking.
Am I mentally sound?

I ran
a hundred miles,
bare feet harshly hitting the ground.
My skin soaked in wind.
My ears soaked in sound.
A hundred miles,
a hundred-mile drive
as music blared.
At least I felt a little bit alive.

Adrenaline rushed through my veins.
My hair danced in the wind.
I closed my eyes to stop the whirlwind I felt within.

I force-fed myself alphabet soup.
wondering how much to eat till the voice taken would be
returned.

Pain often controls every beginning to our story, but we can
determine whether pain will control our end.

Fourteen years.
They lost their mind.
She disappeared.
He hid his lies.

Fifteen years.
Bottled emotions.
Lighted candles
and numbing potions.

Sixteen candles.
City nights and thorny grounds,
broken wings floating on manufactured clouds.

Seventeen candles,
sweet peach pie
cut with pretty knives
from the house laced in lies.

Eighteen years,
blowing out candles of dread.
Make a wish,
eighteen wishes,
but they only had one instead.

As a child, I dreamed in color.
I dreamed of blue skies.
My soul wrapped in innocence,
my hands touched the sky,
my skin soaked in colors,
fluorescent in my mind.

Candied skies,
drizzled in syrup,
sugar-coated my eyes.

As a child, I dreamed in color.
I dreamed of chromatic stars and light.
And in these moments, I thought I was fully alive.

VOLUME 3

THE HOPE

She thought of herself as everything except beauty.
She was a storm, seething within a raindrop.
A waterless rose, thirsting for water in spring.
A forlorn heart, smashed in pieces.
A wildflower, endlessly tumbling in the wind.

But when she reached within her soul,
she found beauty among ashes.

Hatred to self-acceptance,
loyalty, though she had been shown none.
With enchantment rooted within her lungs,
she realized without wounds, how would she have built the
strength to overcome?

As she looked at her future,
all she could see
were broken cages, freed birds,

and an eternity of possibility.

I stopped being a pillow for others to cry on,
a mattress for many people's stunts and falls,
a punching bag for sullen fist,
a target for darted words, shot off of arrowed tongues.
Instead I learned to first take care of myself,
to treat my wounds like a child who had skinned their knee.
Take baby steps to self-love because it does not always come
immediately.
Self-love is a locket,
a reminder hung around the neck,
but self-forgiveness was where I found the key to unlock the
necklace that I kept.

My biggest fear was loneliness,
but soon I realized the toxic souls that surrounded me
were making me feel more alone.

If you're surrounded by nothing good,
separate yourself, and in this you will begin to comprehend true
love—
true love for others and most importantly yourself.

Who taught you that you were not beautiful?
That struggle was shameful?
That wounds made you not enough?
The most beautiful people are the ones that still have pure
hearts even after their souls are crushed.
You are beautiful, not because you have achieved society's
fatuous standards of desired beauty.
You are beautiful because your inner beauty does shine,
taking broken mirrors,
making them utterly divine.

You are beautiful because your soul is watered in fields of
flowers.
Your eyes show that there is always beauty in the midst of
ashes.

So know that with a golden soul like this,
many do not deserve what your heart has to offer,
but you deserve everything you desire,
everything the world has to give,
anything that will give you true happiness.

Many are deceived, to believe that they owe something.
That in order to get what they want, they must give
something up.
You do not owe anything to anyone.
Not now.
Not ever.
If anything, others owe you
for trying to take something that was never theirs.

You owe nothing.

We are all human,
living souls,
living minds,
faded by the idea of perfection,
constantly seeking the remedy that will make us feel whole.

Learn to accept yourself,
because you will end up in tears, with broken limbs and dirt in
your mouth,
trying to be accepted by others.

Instead let in the people who allow you to be you,
because real people are often one in a million,
but when you find them, they will give you a lifetime of
happiness.

Why do bad people attach to those who are good?
Drawing light from you,
mimicking your ways,
telling you sweet lies, they know will draw you closer.

I did not realize this until now, but
bad people attach to you
because you have solidity
something they will never have.
And if they can win by taking this from you,
they will feel better about how dark they are themselves.
So do not spend your time with people who will take what they
need from you, never return it, and then leave.

And don't be fooled.

Ugly things can be clothed in beauty.

When the words *I love you* are used as manipulation,
spoken to bring vulnerability and provoke guilty emotion,
it is associated with shallow minds, cunning souls, and foolish
youth.
So when it is real, you will know.
You will know for sure.

Sometimes to find something better, you must break.

They are just a person,
with crooked words and a daunting smile.

But you, my love, are the world,
the constellations,
the galaxy.

So don't settle for something that isn't worthy of the stars you
hold within.

You could be their ocean.
Grab them out of deep waters and
place them on dry land.

Lift their wings by flight.
Take them to higher sands.

But my dear, don't you understand?
The ocean dances across your fingertips. You have power in
your hands.

And they are not worthy of what your soul has to offer.

Don't run away from someone because you are afraid they
will hurt you.
Just like hurt brought you lessons,
know that new beginnings
bring beautiful flowers, fresh water, and new rains.
So don't run away because you may be missing out on
something that will make you free.

Try to be better than the person who was not good to you.
If your mother hurt you, promise you will be the best mother you can.
If you father is distant, know that you will never distance yourself from the ones you love.
If someone hurts you, know that this was their affliction, and there will be places, people, moments, and time where all those hurts will not matter anymore.

You are better

Be firm in saying no to toxic people who try to slip back into your life.
You have moved too far to ever go back to that place again.

Broken things may never be fixed,
but broken seams always shine light.

At times, you cannot live because life is worth living.
You must live because if you don't,
you will not see what is ahead.

These are lessons I have learned.

Trains passed by,
vivid in my mind.

New York City.
New York City trains.
Doors slide.
Watch your step.
I step towards the train.

Shivers of cold.
I will be gone forever.

Frozen lips
Knit caps.
Heads close together.

I step on the train.
Doors close.
Two different worlds,

I watch you stand on the other side.

I force my hand up.
I wave good-bye,
knowing I will be gone forever.

You smell like fleeting moments,
haunting memories,
fresh flowers.
Though memories stayed etched in my mind,
I knew that I did not want them anymore,
because those memories dragged me from heaven to hell
with you.

You twirled your finger around their hair
looking at them nervously,
Though the walls you had built to block emotion had fallen,
they
were not enough for them to stay down.

Hesitant vulnerability oozed from my mouth.

I had never been the girl with common sense.
The girl satisfied with falsified beings.
The girl who sought attention when she walked in a room.
The girl who held her head as high as a queen,
pride so radiant, people sought it with envy.
But I am the girl,
the girl who sings blue well.
When I hurt, I closed in.
When I felt angry, I destroyed myself.
When I felt alone, I cried hot tears
of ugly self-shame.
When I cared,
I cared too much,
and for that I am to blame.
When I was happy,
I felt as high, one with God in the sky.
Laced-up sneakers
running wild,
swinging hips,
laughing, like an innocent child.
I am the girl,
the girl who spills way too much, always closing my mouth so I don't
open up.
I am the girl
who fakes and pretends,
allowing only few to know who I truly am.
I am the girl,
afraid to trust.
hesitant to smile, because smiles brought pain that stayed for a while.
I am the girl,
dignified yet uncrowned.

I will not lie. My past once did hold me down.
But through this,
I am now the girl who stops at nothing to chase my dreams.
I am passionate for change.
And I do believe
that everyone deserves to be completely free.
I had never been normal.
Normal would have saved a lot of pain.
But I realized this was my magic. It is what made me different.
It is what made me who I am.

Instead of falling in love with broken beings, broken souls,
spinning nights,
and hopeless song,
I decided this time I would fall in love with myself.

I fell in love with blood-stained pages,
written words that came to life.
I fell in love with new places, new people, new beginnings.
I fell in love with forgiveness, knowing that self-forgiveness
begat self-love.
I fell in love with creating myself, caring for myself, watching
myself fall,
loving myself enough to get back up.
I fell in love with who I was, who I was now, who I was
beginning to be.
And in this I took a step toward being completely free.

Forest and skies, surround my eyes.
I finally can breathe, I say with a sigh.
Cut the ropes that leave my feet tied.
Hands unfastened to the sky.

I run free.

For the first time in a while,
forest dreams keep me feeling worthwhile.

I stood in fields of gray,
rewatching my life,
like a movie on replay.

The patterns, the ups, the good moments, the downs,
the rollercoaster of thoughts, the lifeless breaths, the hopeless
sounds.

I smiled and laughed, not because life was a joke
but because in spite of these moments,
I made the decision to fly.

Because without wounds, how would you possess power?
Power to change your destiny.
Eyes to see the broken.
Hands to heal others wounds.
Feet once incapacitated, now used to run across oceans.

The mind that once destroyed, now used to change the world.
I laughed because there were so many more good things to
come.

Though my wings lie placant on the ground I knew that soon I
would fly.

Swaying trees,
and soft green.
Sunsets and skies of luminosity and pink.
Laying down unhazed,
no longer in a maze.
What colors should I paint?
With bruised lips, they whispered,
"Paint me blue."

In remembrance of the color many used to be.

Though thoughts raced through my mind,
I felt frustrated as tears flowed out of my eyes.
I knew that things would get better,
and sometimes it takes time.

As I painted colors on my easel,
I thought,

One day I will look like the colors I once used to be.

Things I thought were irreplaceable.
You.
Thoughts.
Bad moments.
Sadness.
Pain.
But all of these things began to fade
when I opened my eyes to the world of colors and possibilities
ahead.

People are like museums of art.
Each has a past,
a story we sometimes cannot see,
because as people we have learned that vulnerability is a negative thing.
So instead we see paintings of external color,
created to best express who we have become or sometimes what the world wants us to be.

If someone knocks out every living color that dwells inside
of you,
know that to find yourself again, you must erase them from your
canvas and search for the colors you want to be.
But know also that sometimes it takes longer to build a
masterpiece.

Rains
in the middle of July.
Rains are filling my mind.
I jump in the puddles.
I let myself go
because pain isn't meant to be hidden.

Why do you swim in shallow waters, as some drown in the sea?
Swim over to their side,
grab their hand,
set them free.

Do not desensitize the pain.
Do not keep living broken, like they say.

Lips drip in lies,
instead of hungry ears.
I decided this time
to speak out truth,
not only to others but also to myself.

The world is still learning.

We all are still learning.
I am still learning.
So find peace in knowing,

you are not alone.

Hey! You made it. Thank you for taking this journey with me. I hope my words bring you comfort and encouragement in knowing you are not alone. In our society today, we need change—change from the way we create a persona of fear regarding certain topics and issues that are prevalent and affect many in our world today. We need awareness and sensitivity, being aware that we never know what others are going through in their lives. I hope that we will eventually create a community that doesn't shy away from vulnerability, and as a writer, I hope I can contribute a small step toward change and comfortability when talking about society's most sensitive issues. I care, and whatever you are struggling with, remember that you have the strength to get through it. If you need anything, reach out. I am here for you.

With love,
Lauren Mackenzie

If you would like to contact the author you may email her at:
laurenmackenzzie@gmail.com

Printed in the United States
By Bookmasters